# About Skill Builders Grammar

## by Isabelle McCoy, M.Ed., and Leland Graham, Ph.D.

Welcome to RBP Books' Skill Builders series. Like our Summer Bridge Activities collection, the Skill Builders series is designed to make learning both fun and rewarding.

Based on NCTE (National Council of Teachers of English) standards and core curriculum, this grade 6 workbook uses a variety of fun and challenging exercises to teach and reinforce basic grammar concepts. Exercises are grade appropriate, teacher created, and classroom tested, with clear directions and examples to introduce new concepts. As students complete the exercises and games, they will learn about parts of speech, verb tense, subject-verb agreement, sentence types, capitalization, diagramming, punctuation, contractions, and words such as antonyms and synonyms that often give students trouble.

A creative thinking skills section lets students have some fun with language while testing out their new knowledge.

Learning is more effective when approached with an element of fun and enthusiasm—just as most children approach life. That's why the Skill Builders combine entertaining and academically sound exercises with eye-catching graphics and fun themes—to make reviewing basic skills at school or home fun and effective, for both you and your budding scholars.

# Table of Contents

A **noun** names a person, place, or thing. A noun can name specific or general persons, places, or things. Remember: nouns can also name ideas.

Directions: Underline each noun in the narrative that follows.

## Bears

A bear is a big, strong animal with thick, shaggy fur. Bears are classified by scientists as carnivores. Carnivores are animals that mainly eat meat. Bears prey on other animals. They also eat other foods such as nuts, insects, leaves, fish, and fruit. They hunt mice, ground squirrels, and other small animals in fields and forests.

Most wild bears are found north of the equator. They can be found on the continents of Asia, Europe, and North America. Bears can also be found in the Arctic near the North Pole. The spectacled bear is the only species living in South America. No wild bears live in Australia, Antarctica, or Africa.

A bear prepares for its winter sleep, or hibernation, by eating large amounts of food in late summer and by storing fat within its body. In the winter, when food becomes scarce, the bear goes into its den. Some bears spend much of the winter in a state similar to sleeping. Some bears in areas with mild winters may enter their dens for only a short time.

1

# Nouns as Subjects

Nouns can function as the **subject** of a sentence. In order to decide if a word is the subject, ask the question *Who?* or *What?* followed by the verb. In most sentences, the verb follows the subject.

**Example:** <u>Randall</u> mows the yard every Friday.
(Who mows?)

Directions: Underline the noun that is the subject in the following sentences.

1. Parrots are noisy birds that live mainly in forested areas.

2. Strong, grasping feet enable parrots to hang acrobatically from tree branches.

3. *Parakeet* is the general name for many types of small to medium-sized parrots.

4. Common foods of parrots include fruits, nuts, seeds, and buds.

5. The United States once had its own species of parrots.

6. The Carolina parakeet became extinct around 1920 because of forest destruction and hunting.

7. Macaws are large parrots that live mostly in the tropical forests of South America.

8. Parrotlets are tiny parakeets that have short tails.

Nouns

# Nouns as Predicate Nominatives

A **predicate nominative** is a noun or pronoun that follows a linking verb. It renames or gives more information about the subject. It also answers the question *Who?* or *What is?* The linking verb describes a condition, not an action.

Example: A turtle is a reptile with a shell.

Directions: Circle the subject. Underline the predicate nominative once and label it **PN**; then underline the linking verb twice and label it **LV**.

1. Subir is a foreign exchange student at the university.

2. Harriet Tubman was a former slave who worked on the Underground Railroad.

3. Mrs. Allen is the principal of Henderson Middle School.

4. Jasmine and Tiera were partners at the skating meet.

5. I am captain of the Browns Mill softball team.

6. The Atlanta Thrashers is the hockey team that I support.

7. Mark will be the president of the sixth grade class.

8. John Glenn became an astronaut with the NASA space program.

9. My brother is a computer analyst with a large corporation.

10. Veronica is a student in my social studies class.

# Common and Proper Nouns

A **proper noun** names a particular person, place, idea, or thing. A **common noun** does not name a particular person, place, idea, or thing.

| Common | Proper |
|---|---|
| dog | German shepherd |
| day | Wednesday |
| street | Charles Avenue |
| building | Empire State Building |

Directions: Write a common or proper noun for each word in the blanks below.

| Common | Proper |
|---|---|
| **1.** boy | **1.** _____ |
| **2.** desert | **2.** _____ |
| **3.** _____ | **3.** Mary Catherine |
| **4.** country | **4.** _____ |
| **5.** _____ | **5.** Mt. Everest |
| **6.** dessert | **6.** _____ |
| **7.** language | **7.** _____ |
| **8.** teacher | **8.** _____ |
| **9.** _____ | **9.** Amazon |
| **10.** capital | **10.** _____ |
| **11.** _____ | **11.** Spanish |
| **12.** war | **12.** _____ |
| **13.** city | **13.** _____ |

# Singular and Plural Nouns

Most nouns form their **plurals** by adding -s or -es. Other plurals are formed in special ways; however, some nouns do not change at all.

**Example:** dog—dogs (add -s)
church—churches (add -es)
baby—babies (change y to i and add -es)
moose—moose (no change at all)
woman—women (change in spelling)

Directions: Add the singular or plural form to complete the chart.

| Singular | Plural |
|---|---|
| **1.** can | **1.** |
| **2.** dish | **2.** |
| **3.** | **3.** mice |
| **4.** | **4.** babies |
| **5.** chair | **5.** |
| **6.** | **6.** bunches |
| **7.** party | **7.** |
| **8.** box | **8.** |
| **9.** | **9.** deer |
| **10.** | **10.** children |
| **11.** calf | **11.** |
| **12.** trout | **12.** |
| **13.** potato | **13.** |
| **14.** | **14.** men |

 Grammar Grade 6—RBP013X

# Singular and Plural Possessive Nouns

A **possessive noun** shows ownership. Form the possessive of a **singular noun** by adding apostrophe (') and -s.

**Example:**  girl**'s** dress    Mrs. Davis**'s** car

Form the possessive of a **plural noun** that ends in -s by adding only an apostrophe (').

**Example:**  dog**s'** tails    girl**s'** purses

Form the possessive of a **plural noun** that does not end in -s by adding an apostrophe (') and -s.

**Example:**  the men**'s** cars    children**'s** toys

Directions: Choose the correct possessive form of the noun for the following sentences.

1. _____ math book has been missing for days.
   A. Vanessas'    B. Vanessa's    C. Vanessa'

2. The _____ club met weekly to discuss the community flower garden.
   A. women's    B. womens'    C. womens's

3. Did you know that _____ house is located near the mall?
   A. Janis's    B. Janis'    C. Janis

4. The _____ pups were learning to stalk prey.
   A. wolf's    B. wolfs'    C. wolfs's

5. Those _____ flags were all up, indicating there was mail.
   A. mailboxes'    B. mailboxes's    C. mailboxes

6. Mr. _____ family is having a reunion next month.
   A. Jone's    B. Jones'    C. Jones's

# Identifying Pronouns and Their Antecedents

A **pronoun** is a word that is used as a substitute for, or instead of, a noun. The noun a pronoun refers to (or takes the place of) is called its **antecedent**. Commonly used pronouns include *I, me, he, him, she, her, it, you, your, they, them, their, we, us, our, my,* and *mine.*

**Example:** Ann has given **her** permission to publish the book.
(*her* = pronoun; *Ann* = antecedent)

She wants to earn royalties for **it**.
(*it* = pronoun; *book* = antecedent)

Directions: In the following sentences, underline the pronouns once. Then, whenever possible, indicate the antecedent to a pronoun by underlining it twice.

1. Keith swam in the Olympic-size pool until he became exhausted.

2. The boys enjoyed racing on their bikes during the summer.

3. I sang for three years in the chorus at my middle school.

4. The refrigerator's motor needed oil in order for it to run smoothly.

5. The Smith family enjoyed their vacation in Yosemite National Park, and they took many pictures.

6. Your dog's continual barking is keeping me from sleeping at night.

7. Do you know Mr. Thomas and his nephew Brian?

# Subject and Object Pronouns

A **subject pronoun** is used as the subject or as part of the subject of a sentence. Subject pronouns are *I, you, she, he, it, they,* and *we.* (When the pronoun *I* is used with other pronouns or with nouns, it is always named last.)

**Example:** **We** enjoyed the movie last night.

An **object pronoun** is used after an action verb or a preposition, such as *for, from, in, of, to, with, except, after between, at,* or *against.* The object pronouns are *you, me, her, him, it, us,* and *them.* (When the pronoun *me* is used with other pronouns or nouns, it is always named last.)

**Example:** The birthday present was given to **him**.

Directions: Choose the correct pronoun in each sentence and label it as a subject pronoun *(SUBJ.)* or as an object pronoun *(OBJ.)*.

**1.** Jane's father purchased a new video game for (she, her).

**2.** Laney and (I, me) wanted the new CD for our collection.

**3.** Diedre asked (they, them) to go with her to the concert.

**4.** (He, Him) told the class about his trip to Disney World.

**5.** Jeffrey is showing (we, us) how to make origami animals.

**6.** Juan and (I, me) are going to the post office to mail the package.

**7.** (She, You) have a beautiful house and family.

**8.** The box was found in the basement near (it, we).

8

# Possessive Pronouns

A **possessive pronoun** is one that shows ownership or possession. Possessive pronouns include *his, her, hers, its, our, ours, my, mine, your, yours, their,* and *theirs.*

**Example:** Manuel lost **his** watch at the beach.
*(His is the possessive pronoun, modifying watch.)*

Directions: In the following sentences, underline the possessive pronoun and then draw an arrow to the noun that it modifies.

1. Carmen and her father drove to the beach house.

2. Did you know that your CD is in the laundry room?

3. This painting by Rembrandt is like the one in our library.

4. Do you know how Atlanta acquired its name?

5. Their mother was calling to say that dinner was ready.

6. My brother and sister both attended a private school.

7. The huge mess in the den is yours, not Tony's.

8. Are the brown shoes under the table mine?

9. Our teacher told the class about the test tomorrow.

10. His softball team is going to be in the finals.

11. Your geography book has a chapter on Mongolia.

12. Where in the world are her glasses?

# Identifying Adjectives

An **adjective** describes or modifies a noun or pronoun by telling *which one*, *what kind*, or *how many*. The adjectives *a*, *an*, and *the* are called **articles**.

**Example:** *Which one*—**Those** toys belong to Jonathan.

*What kind*—The **big, green** frog jumped high.

*How many*—**Most** children enjoy riding a bike.

*Articles*—**The** computer is on **a** table in **the** hall.

Directions: Underline the adjectives in the following story. Can you find all the adjectives in the narrative?

A tarantula is the common name of a group of large hairy spiders. Tarantulas are found in warm climates such as the southern and western United States and in the Tropics. Some tarantulas may live twenty years or more. The name *tarantula* comes from a wolf spider found near Taranto, Italy.

One of the world's largest spiders is the *bird spider*. Found in South America, it is a type of tarantula. Some bird spiders live in the trees and eat small birds. In Brazil there are some tarantulas that eat small reptiles and amphibians.

Tarantulas found in the U.S. are quiet creatures that live in burrows. The main way these tarantulas have to defend themselves is to fling thousands of microscopic, irritating body hairs into the air by rubbing motions of the hind legs. The bite of these tarantulas is no more dangerous to people than a bee sting.

Can you find 41?

# Indefinite Pronouns and Demonstrative Adjectives

An **indefinite pronoun** is one that tells an approximate number or quantity. It does not tell exactly how many or how much. Some indefinite pronouns include *all*, *anybody*, *each*, *few*, *many*, *more*, *most*, *several*, and *some*.

**Example:** **Some** of those dishes on the counter are cracked.

A **demonstrative adjective** points out a particular person, place, or thing. Demonstrative adjectives include *this*, *that*, *these*, and *those*. *This* and *that* are singular. *These* and *those* are plural. Use *this* and *these* for things close by. Use *that* and *those* for things that are distant in time or space.

**Example:** **This** blouse does not match the skirt.

Directions: Circle the indefinite pronoun(s) or demonstrative adjective(s) in the following sentences.

1. These science books were found in the hallway.

2. Does anybody know where my science book is?

3. This camera belongs to my older brother Nathaniel.

4. I have found that bracelet Mother gave you.

5. I lived in Germany for a few years before I moved to the United States.

6. Do you have any ideas for decorating the cafeteria?

7. How many of those horses have you ridden this year?

8. Several times a week my parents check my homework.

11

# Comparative and Superlative Adjectives

When adjectives are used to compare people, places, or things, there are certain spelling rules to follow.

1. For most adjectives, add -er or -est to the end.

   small          smaller          smallest

2. For adjectives with a consonant preceded by a single vowel, double the final consonant and add -er or -est.

   thin           thinner          thinnest

3. For adjectives ending in e, drop the e and add -er or -est.

   wide           wider            widest

4. For adjectives that end in a y preceded by a consonant, change the y to i and add -er or -est.

   tiny           tinier           tiniest

5. For adjectives of more than two syllables, add the word *more* in front of the adjective to form the comparative degree. To form the superlative degree, add the word *most* in front of the adjective.

Directions: Complete the following chart using the rules of comparative and superlative degrees listed above.

| Adjective | Add -er | Add -est |
|---|---|---|
| **1.** green | | |
| **2.** tardy | | |
| **3.** sweet | | |
| **4.** strong | | |
| **5.** happy | | |
| **6.** beautiful | | |
| **7.** stinky | | |
| **8.** thankful | | |
| **9.** important | | |
| **10.** colorful | | |
| **11.** little | | |
| **12.** angry | | |

# Predicate Adjectives

A **predicate adjective** (also called a subject complement) modifies the subject, but it must follow a linking verb (see the list below) in the sentence. These verbs are linking verbs only if they are followed by an adjective, noun, or pronoun that renames the subject.

Most common linking verbs are forms of the verb *to be:*
*is, are, was, were, am, being, been*

Other linking verbs include the following:
*appear, become, feel, grow, look, prove, remain, seem, smell, sound, stand, taste, turn*

**Example:** The red <u>apples</u> are **sweet**. (sweet apples)

The <u>milk</u> has turned **sour**. (sour milk)

Directions: In the following sentences, underline the predicate adjectives. Draw an arrow to the subject (noun or pronoun) that it modifies.

**1.** The female singer was extremely talented.

**2.** The watermelon tasted delicious on this hot summer day.

**3.** Cynthia looks beautiful in that yellow dress.

**4.** Gardenias smell wonderful on a warm June day.

**5.** Kenneth seems tired after swimming in the meet.

**6.** The children are angry because our trip to the beach was cancelled.

**7.** Nelsey grew impatient as she waited for her mother.

# Identifying Verbs

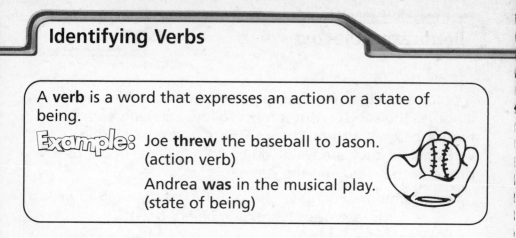

A **verb** is a word that expresses an action or a state of being.

**Example:** Joe **threw** the baseball to Jason. (action verb)

Andrea **was** in the musical play. (state of being)

Directions: In the following passage, underline all the verbs.

Louisa May Alcott was an American author. *Little Women*, her best-known book, tells the story of four sisters growing up in New England. Ms. Alcott also worked to gain voting rights for women.

Alcott was born in Germantown, Pennsylvania, but she grew up in Boston and Concord, Massachusetts. Her father was a philosopher and an educational reformer. Many of the family's friends and neighbors were well-known writers, such as Nathaniel Hawthorne and Henry David Thoreau. All of these people influenced Louisa.

Ms. Alcott spent most of her childhood in poverty because her father invested money in many projects that failed. She began to help support the family at an early age by working as a seamstress, a household servant, and a teacher.

Her first book, *Flower Fables*, consisted of fairy stories that she made up to tell one of her students. Her first novel, *Moods*, was published in 1864. In 1867 she became the editor of *Merry's Museum*, a magazine for girls.

14

# Action and Linking Verbs

An **action verb** is a word that shows action. That action could be something that you cannot see. An action verb tells what the subject does.

**Example:** Micah **dribbled** the basketball down the court.

A **linking verb** links the subject with a word or words in the predicate. Common linking verbs include *am*, *appear*, *are*, *is*, *feel*, *look*, *seem*, *smell*, *taste*, *was*, and *were*.

**Example:** The cover of the book **looks** exciting.

Directions: Underline the verb(s) in the following sentences. Label each action verb *(AV)* and each linking verb *(LV)*.

**1.** One of the largest cities in Colorado is Pueblo.

**2.** The city of Pueblo lies at the junction of the Arkansas River and Fountain Creek.

**3.** Pueblo is the home of the University of Southern Colorado.

**4.** Since 1872 the city has hosted the annual Colorado State Fair.

**5.** Arapaho, Cheyenne, and Ute Indians lived in eastern Colorado.

**6.** In 1840 trappers built Fort Pueblo on the site of what is now the city of Pueblo.

**7.** The Utes killed the fort's inhabitants in 1854.

15

A **transitive verb** shows action passing from a doer to a receiver. A transitive verb has a direct object. An **intransitive verb** is one which has no receiver of its action. The subject is the doer of the action.

**Example:** Jennifer **washed** her new car. (*transitive*)

Jennifer **washed** today. (*intransitive*)

Directions: In the following sentences underline the main verb. Label each verb transitive *(T)* or intransitive *(IN)*.

1. Joshua ate the rib-eye steak for supper.

2. The kitten meowed all night long.

3. Mr. Todd instructed the class on the proper way to divide decimals.

4. My Aunt Beverly sang a song in the musical.

5. Everett is a very skilled carpenter in my neighborhood.

6. Carlos and Miguel love their new skateboards.

7. Carlos and Miguel raced on their new skateboards.

8. The waitress ignored the impatient customers.

9. Our science teacher assigned a project that is due on Friday.

10. They have written several science assignments.

11. The crickets were chirping all night long.

# Verb Tenses: Present, Past, and Future

The three basic **verb tenses** are **present**, **past**, and **future**.

*Present tense* verbs show action that is *happening now*.
**Example:** We **talk** on the telephone. (action verb)
Ariel **is** a telephone operator. (linking verb)

*Past tense* verbs show action that *happened earlier*.
**Example:** Ashley **talked** on the telephone.
Al **was** a telephone operator.

*Future tense* verbs show action that *will happen*.
**Example:** Walter **will talk** on the telephone.
Edward **will be** a telephone operator.

Directions: Underline the verb(s) in the following sentences and then identify the tense by writing *PR* for present, *PS* for past, or *F* for future on the line provided.

1. _____ The play was cancelled because of the snowstorm.

2. _____ Will you come to the mall with me this afternoon?

3. _____ Jarrod is walking his dog around the block.

4. _____ Sonny will work on my computer tomorrow evening.

5. _____ Yesterday I finished writing my book report.

6. _____ Your red jacket is on the stage in the cafeteria.

7. _____ Sarah Ann has the recipe for those cookies.

8. _____ Aunt Martha and Uncle Tony enjoyed their visit.

9. _____ Every day the sixth grade class says the Pledge of Allegiance.

# Perfect Verb Tenses

The **present perfect tense** places an action or condition in a time period leading up to the present.

**Example:** Computers **have existed** for more than 50 years.

The **past perfect tense** places a past action or condition before another past action or condition.

**Example:** After office workers **had used** computers for years, they discovered their usefulness at home.

The **future perfect tense** places a future action or condition before another future action or condition.

**Example:** Many more office workers **will have used** computers at work than at their homes.

Directions: In the following sentences, identify the perfect tense(s) of the underlined verbs by writing the tense in the blank.

**1.** Alice <u>will have finished</u> her science project before it is due.

_____

**2.** The race car drivers <u>had driven</u> in many races.

_____

**3.** I <u>have enjoyed</u> cooking breakfast each day.

_____

**4.** Amy <u>had finished</u> her assignments for the week.

_____

**5.** Do you think he <u>will have graded</u> our papers by tomorrow? _____

# Identifying Adverbs

> An **adverb** describes or modifies a verb, an adjective, or another adverb. Many but not all adverbs end with -*ly*.
>
> **Example:** Baseball practice <u>will end</u> **soon**.
> (*soon* modifies the verb *will end*)
>
> The **very** <u>difficult</u> test lasted three hours.
> (*very* modifies the adjective *difficult*)
>
> The sports car drove **extremely** <u>fast</u>.
> (*extremely* modifies the adverb *fast*)

Directions: Read the following passage and underline all of the adverbs.

A bird of prey is described as a very large bird that usually hunts small animals. Birds of prey have extremely strong curved bills and very strong claws. They are also known as raptors. These birds feed mainly on other vertebrate animals, especially mammals. These birds are primarily predatory but many include carrion or dead animals in their diet. Some feed only on dead animals.

The features common to this group of birds include a very mighty hooked beak. The legs are short and extremely powerful. All of the toes have large, sharply pointed and curved claws. These birds' vision is particularly acute, and the sense of smell seems to be better developed in carrion-eaters than the others.

©RBP Books                Grammar Grade 6—RBP013X

An **adverb** answers questions such as *how*, *when*, *where*, and *how much*. It can describe what time, place, cause, degree, or in what manner. Some adverbs can be identified by their characteristic *-ly* suffix. Most must be identified by understanding the grammatical relationships within a sentence. An adverb, unlike an adjective, can be found in various places within a sentence.

**Example:** Did you **really** have fun at school?
(adverb within)

Grandma went home **today**.
(adverb at the end)

**Now** we need to wash.
(adverb at the beginning)

Directions: Underline the adverb(s) in the following sentences.

1. This summer we are going to swim daily.

2. Very early each morning we will take lessons and learn many new strokes.

3. Throughout the long, hot summer we expect to work extremely hard.

4. Tennis player Serena Williams will probably win Wimbledon this year.

5. Tennis is most difficult for people who are not in good physical shape.

6. Darius truly enjoys playing soccer for the local YMCA.

7. Luis has been thoroughly enjoying his summer job of mowing lawns.

8. The Davidson family reunion always occurs in August.

9. Summertime was usually fun when I was a young child, and it is still fun today.

20

# Comparing Adverbs

Most adverbs, like adjectives, show comparison when the word endings *-er* and *-est* are added to them.

When adverbs compare two actions, add *-er*, or add *more* if the adverb ends in *-ly* or is more than one syllable.

When adverbs compare three or more actions, add *-est*, or add *most* if the adverb ends in *-ly* or has more than two syllables.

Adverb with one action:
Monique arrived **late**.

Adverb comparing two actions:
Monique arrived **later** than Nathan.

Adverb comparing three or more actions:
Monique arrived **latest** of all

Directions: Choose the correct form of the adverb in parentheses.

**1.** This was the (better, best) movie I have seen.

**2.** The math test was (harder, hardest) than the science test.

**3.** Frederick learned (good, well) from his mistakes.

**4.** Adrienne was (less patient, least patient) than Arthur.

**5.** Marcia plays (more skillfully, most skillfully) of all the students.

**6.** Of the students, Michele was the (slower, slowest).

**7.** Coco behaved (more calmly, most calmly) of all the puppies.

**8.** This tuna casserole is the (worse, worst) I've eaten.

21

# Adjective or Adverb?

Directions: For each underlined word circle the letter that correctly identifies it as an adjective or adverb.

Music is sound arranged into (1) <u>pleasing</u> or interesting patterns. It forms a (2) <u>very</u> important part of many activities.

People (3) <u>usually</u> use music to express feelings and ideas.

Music is one of the (4) <u>oldest</u> arts. People (5) <u>probably</u> started to sing as soon as language began. (6) <u>Many</u> ancient peoples used music in religious ceremonies. The (7) <u>first</u> music that was written dates from around 2500 B.C.

**1.** A. adverb modifying *into*
   B. adverb modifying *is*
   C. adjective modifying *patterns*
   D. adverb modifying *sound*

**2.** A. adjective modifying *forms*
   B. adjective modifying *important*
   C. adverb modifying *important*
   D. adverb modifying *part*

**3.** A. adverb modifying *use*
   B. adverb modifying *music*
   C. adjective modifying *use*
   D. adjective modifying *music*

**4.** A. adverb modifying *arts*
   B. adverb modifying *one*
   C. adjective modifying *arts*
   D. adjective modifying *one*

**5.** A. adjective modifying *people*
   B. adjective modifying *started*
   C. adverb modifying *sing*
   D. adverb modifying *started*

**6.** A. adjective modifying *ancient*
   B. adjective modifying *music*
   C. adjective modifying *peoples*
   D. adverb modifying *started*

**7.** A. adverb modifying *written*
   B. adverb modifying *music*
   C. adjective modifying *written*
   D. adjective modifying *music*

www.summerbridgeactivities.com

# Adjectival and Adverbial Phrases

An **adjectival phrase**, which begins with a preposition, is a group of words used as an **adjective**.

**Example:** The siege **of the Alamo** lasted thirteen days.
*(of the Alamo* modifies *siege)*

An **adverbial phrase** is a group of words used as an **adverb**. A preposition begins an adverbial phrase.

**Example:** A famous battle was fought there **from February 23** to March 6, 1836.
*(from February 23* modifies *was fought)*

Directions: Identify each underlined adjectival and adverbial phrase. On the line, write *ADJ.* or *ADV.* to identify what kind of phrase it is. Then circle the word it modifies.

1. _____ No Texans escaped <u>from the Alamo</u> after the night of March 5.

2. _____ The Alamo, built as a Roman Catholic mission, was established <u>in San Antonio</u> in 1718.

3. _____ It was called the *Alamo* because of the Spanish name <u>for the cottonwood trees</u> surrounding the mission.

4. _____ During the winter of 1835–1836, the people of Texas decided to sever their relations <u>with Mexico</u>.

5. _____ Lt. Colonel William Travis and a force <u>of 150 Texans</u> sought to defend the city.

6. _____ <u>At the end</u>, the Texans fought using their rifles as clubs.

© RBP Books

# Identifying Prepositions

A **preposition** is a word used to show the relationship of a noun or a pronoun to some other word in the sentence. A preposition is placed before a noun or pronoun that becomes the object of the preposition. Some commonly used prepositions are as follows:

| | | | |
|---|---|---|---|
| about | below | in | over |
| above | behind | near | through |
| across | during | on | to |
| after | except | of | under |
| around | for | off | with |
| before | from | out | without |

Directions: Underline the preposition(s) in the following sentences.

1. During lunch I always talk with my friends.

2. The school bus stopped in front of my house today.

3. The flavor of root beer comes partly from the spicy bark of the root of the sassafras.

4. After many fatiguing hours of flight, we arrived in Paris.

5. Under the desk is where you will find my brother's shoes.

6. Mexican jumping beans are sold in novelty shops.

7. A flock of pigeons circled overhead during the concert.

8. The attractive woman in the red dress is my neighbor.

9. The frightened rabbit leaped through a narrow opening in the fence.

# Prepositional Phrases as Adjectives or Adverbs

A **prepositional phrase** that modifies a noun or pronoun is an **adjective phrase**. A **prepositional phrase** that modifies a verb, adjective, or adverb is an **adverb phrase**.

**Example:** The airports **in Miami and Chicago** are crowded.
*(in Miami and Chicago* = adjective phrase, modifying *airports)*

Paul threw the ball far **to the left**.
*(to the left* = adverb phrase, modifying *far)*

Directions: Underline the prepositional phrase(s). Write *ADJ.* if the phrase is an adjectival prepositional phrase. Write *ADV.* if the phrase is an adverbial prepositional phrase.

1. The arch in St. Louis is a well-known landmark.

2. The new mayor of Atlanta discussed many of the traffic problems.

3. The members of the club want sweatshirts with the club emblem.

4. The scouting party listened silently to the captain's instructions.

5. The Indians of the western plains depended on the buffalo for food and clothing.

6. The tiny mountainous country of Andorra lies on the border between France and Spain.

7. In 1783 two Frenchmen flew to a height of five hundred feet in a hot air balloon.

# Conjunctions: Coordinating and Correlative

A **conjunction** is a word that connects words or groups of words. **Coordinating conjunctions**, such as *and, but,* and *or,* connect related words, groups of words, or sentences.

**Example:** Sarah **and** Josh are square dance partners.

**Correlative conjunctions** are conjunctions used in pairs to connect sentence parts. *Either... or, neither... nor, whether... or* are commonly used correlative conjunctions.

**Example:** **Neither** Jan **nor** Sarah wanted to go to the mall.

Directions: As you read the passage on owls, circle each coordinating and correlative conjunction in the paragraph below.

An owl is a type of bird that usually lives alone and hunts for food at night. The owl has been called the night watchman of our gardens because it eats harmful rodents at night. It is a bird of prey, but it is not thought to be closely related to other birds of prey.

Scientists have identified about 145 species of owls. Owls live throughout the tropical, temperate, and subarctic regions of the world, and they can be found on many oceanic islands.

The eyes of most owls are large and are directed forward, unlike the eyes of most other birds. Most night-hunting owls have either keen vision in the dark, or they have such sensitive hearing that they rely very little on vision. But unlike people, owls cannot move their eyes in their sockets. Thus, they must move their heads to watch a moving object.

The smallest owl, the elf, measures about six inches (15 cm) long, but the largest, the great gray owl, measures about 30 inches (76 cm) long.

26

# Conjunctions: Subordinating

**Subordinating conjunctions** are words that begin adverb clauses. Adverb clauses contain subjects and verbs, but do *not* stand alone as sentences. They modify a main clause.

Commonly used subordinating conjunctions are as follows:

| after | before | though | whenever |
|-------|--------|--------|----------|
| although | if | unless | where |
| as | since | until | wherever |
| because | than | when | while |

**Example:** I do not know **when** I have had such a good time.

Directions: As you read the passage on owls, circle each subordinating conjunction in the paragraph below.

Because owls eat mostly mammals, they catch rabbits and squirrels. Owls usually capture their food alive, although sometimes they pick up animals that have been recently killed along highways. Some owls hunt birds and insects, while others have been known to take fish from shallow waters. Like hawks, owls tear large prey into pieces when they eat it. If the prey is small enough, they swallow it whole. Since they cough up pellets of bones, fur, scales, and feathers, which they cannot digest, these pellets can be found under their nests.

Since owls do not build elaborate nests, their nests are usually old nests of hawks or crows. Whenever a female owl lays eggs, there are usually three or four, although some lay as few as one or as many as twelve. The eggs are nearly round and are white with a tinge of blue. Male and female owls care for their nests. Because larger owls defend the nests against intruders, they sometimes injure people by striking with their sharp talons.

# Interjections

An **interjection** is a word or a group of words that express a strong feeling. Interjections do not depend on or relate to any other word(s) in the sentence. An interjection can be followed by an **exclamation mark** if it shows strong feeling and stands alone. On the other hand, if the interjection shows mild feeling, it is followed by a **comma** and begins the sentence.

Example: Ouch! That really hurt.

Ah, that was a job well done.

Directions: Use the following interjections to create a sentence of your own.

1. Whoa! _____

2. Oh! _____

3. Wow! _____

4. Look out! _____

5. Hurray! _____

6. Ah, _____

7. Good grief! _____

8. Great! _____

9. Ouch! _____

10. Beware! _____

# Writing Complete Subjects and Predicates

The **complete subject** contains the simple subject (noun or pronoun) and any other words that tell who or what the sentence is about. The **complete predicate** contains the simple predicate (verb or linking verb) and any other words that describe the actions of the subject or conditions of a subject following a linking verb.

Example:   The red, juicy tomatoes were absolutely delicious.
            CS                          CP

Directions: Complete the following sentences with the missing subject or predicate.

1. Jeffrey and Mark _____.

2. _____ played the drums in the school band.

3. _____ wanted to run for class president.

4. The large gray wolf _____.

5. Angela and her sister _____.

6. _____ was interested in studying archaeology.

7. _____ came to my house to study for the science test.

8. The ice in the refrigerator _____.

9. The final chapter in the book _____.

10. _____ was arrested for the crime.

# Diagramming Simple Sentences

Diagramming creates a picture of a sentence's parts. The most basic diagram is the simple subject and simple predicate. The format of the simple sentence is as follows: <u>simple subject</u> | <u>simple predicate</u>. The vertical line separates the simple subject from the simple predicate.

Step #1: Locate the complete subject and predicate.

Example:

| The beautiful picture | hung on the wall. |
|---|---|
| (complete subject) | (complete predicate) |

Step #2: Narrow down the simple subject and predicate.

Example:

| picture | hung |
|---|---|
| (simple subject) | (predicate) |

Directions: Diagram the simple subject and simple predicate in each of the following sentences.

**1.** The carpet in the hall is dirty.

**2.** An art festival is scheduled in April.

**3.** In the summertime I enjoy swimming in the park.

www.summerbridgeactivities.com                ©RBP Books

## Subject-Verb Agreement

The subject of a sentence must agree with its verb. If the subject is **singular**, use a singular form of the verb. If the subject is **plural**, use a plural form of the verb.

**Singular Subject** — When the subject is a singular noun or *he*, *she*, or *it*, add *s* to the verb.

A doctor **helps** people. He **cures** aches.

**Plural Subject** — When the subject is a plural noun or *I*, *we*, *you*, or *they*, do not add *s* to the verb.

Doctors **help** people. They **cure** aches.

Directions: Circle the correct verb form that agrees with the subject.

1. Arial (sing, sings) with the new rock band.

2. This school (has, have) many interesting students.

3. My mother and father (own, owns) two cars and a motor-cycle.

4. The Parker family (live, lives) in Seattle, Washington.

5. Jeffrey's father (work, works) for the local phone company.

6. They (was, were) planning their summer vacation.

7. Do you (has, have) any money that I can borrow?

8. (Are, Is) you going to the mall tomorrow?

9. How did you (make, makes) those delicious cookies?

A **direct object** is a word or group of words that names the receiver of the action of an action verb. In a typical English sentence, the direct object follows the verb and answers the question *Whom*? or *What*? Generally speaking, the subject of the sentence does something to the direct object.

**Example:** Timothy hung the **painting** in the hall.
(*Hung what?*)

Directions: In each sentence, underline the direct object.

1. Mrs. Jennings offered cookies to the students.

2. The maid washed the dishes in the sink.

3. Harriett presented a door prize to the winner.

4. For the picnic Mrs. Johns made potato salad.

5. All of the sixth grade students passed the math test.

6. Juanita carried the basket on her head.

7. Winston asked Roger about the game.

8. For her birthday Marsha received a camera.

9. The homeless man quickly ate the sandwich.

10. Remember to send a thank-you note.

11. The red bird made a nest in our birch tree.

12. Dorran spent his money on pizza.

# Indirect Objects

An **indirect object** is a word or group of words that tells *to whom* or *for whom* (or *to what* or *for what*) an action is done. The indirect object usually comes between the verb and the direct object. Watch for these verbs that are often followed by an indirect object: *ask*, *bring*, *give*, *lend*, *make*, *made*, *offer*, *send*, *show*, *teach*, *tell*, and *write*.

**Example:** Patrice read the **children** a story.
(To whom did Patrice read the story?)

Directions: Underline the indirect object in the following sentences.

1. Tamara made Harriett a new yellow dress.

2. Matthew showed John the pictures from his trip.

3. Mrs. Cook taught her students some manners.

4. Father gave me a computer for my birthday.

5. The student asked Mrs. Drake a question.

6. Jane offered Denise a piece of chocolate candy.

7. Tracy told her little sister a special secret.

8. Leslie wrote Alicia a story about turtles.

9. Please hand Suzanne the book on space.

10. Angelica made Shawn some oatmeal cookies.

11. The rock music gave Mother a headache.

12. Joseph, will you lend Alvin forty dollars?

Grammar Grade 6—RBP013X

# Diagramming Direct and Indirect Objects

In diagramming, the **direct object** is considered a main sentence part and is placed on the horizontal line with the simple subject and predicate. A vertical line that touches the horizontal line separates the direct object from the verb.

**Example:** For her birthday Marsha received a camera.

| Marsha | received | camera |
|--------|----------|--------|

The **indirect object** is diagrammed beneath the verb on a short horizontal line with a slanting line joining it to the verb.

**Example:** Matthew showed John the pictures from his trip.

| Matthew | showed | pictures |
|---------|--------|----------|
|         | John   |          |

Directions: Diagram each sentence below using the same pattern as shown in the examples. Do *not* add the modifiers.

**1.** My sister Heather likes movies.

**2.** Joseph bought Mary a bracelet.

**3.** Her mistake taught us a costly lesson.

**4.** The actress handed him the sealed envelope.

34

# Kinds of Sentences

Sentences may be classified as **declarative**, **imperative**, **interrogative**, or **exclamatory**.

1. A **declarative sentence** makes a statement and ends with a period (.).

   **Example:** *Romeo and Juliet* was written by Shakespeare**.**

2. An **imperative sentence** gives a command or makes a request and is usually followed by a period (.).

   **Example:** Read *Romeo and Juliet* by Shakespeare.

3. An **interrogative sentence** asks a question and is followed by a question mark (?).

   **Example:** Have you read *Romeo and Juliet*?

4. An **exclamatory sentence** shows strong feeling and is followed by an exclamation mark (!).

   **Example:** What a great play *Romeo and Juliet* is!

Directions: Identify each of the following sentences as *declarative*, *imperative*, *interrogative*, or *exclamatory*. Provide the proper end punctuation.

1. _____ Denise could not finish her science project

2. _____ What a storm that was last night

3. _____ Do you think we will have rain today

4. _____ Take this assignment with you

5. _____ What a scary movie that was

6. _____ May I help you with your activity

7. _____ Open your books to page thirty

8. _____ Jimmy Carter won the Nobel Peace Prize

35

© RBP Books

Grammar Grade 6—RBP013X

# Subjects in Imperative and Interrogative Sentences

**You** is always the **subject** of an **imperative sentence**. Often *you* doesn't appear in the sentence because it is understood.

**Example:** (*You*) Pass your papers to the first person.
(The subject *you* is understood.)

To find the subject in an interrogative sentence, turn the question into a statement. Then ask *who* or *what* is or does something.

**Example:** Did Fred talk with you?
**Fred** did talk with you.
(Who or what did talk? *Fred* is the subject.)

Directions: Write the subject on the line that is provided.

1. _____ Go to the grocery store now.

2. _____ Did Maurice sing in the choir?

3. _____ Was the test in science difficult?

4. _____ Wash your father's car after school.

5. _____ Finish all of your homework before dinner.

6. _____ Will Jonathan teach chemistry next year?

7. _____ Clean your room before you leave.

8. _____ Take out the garbage and wash the dishes.

9. _____ Can Jeffrey participate in the play?

# Compound Sentences

A **compound sentence** is composed of two or more simple sentences joined by a comma and a conjunction.

Example: I want to go to the play, **but** I have to study first.

Directions: Underline each simple sentence and circle the conjunction.

1. Andrew sang in the choir, and he played in the band.

2. I am glad today is Friday, but I have many chores to do.

3. Grandpa ate his dinner, and then he took a nap.

4. Do you want to see a play, or do you want to go to a movie?

5. Jeremy enjoyed the roast, but he didn't care for any of the vegetables.

Directions: Combine the following pairs of sentences with an appropriate coordinating conjunction.

6. The last book I read was *Holes*. I enjoyed the book.

_____

7. Angelina drank the milk. It was very sour.

_____

8. Seventy-five percent of the earth is covered by water. Most of it is salt water.

_____

9. Cats make great pets. Sometimes they scratch my sister.

_____

# Diagramming Compound Subjects and Predicates

Simple sentences can have either a **compound subject** or a **compound predicate**. To diagram a sentence with two subjects or predicates, place the two words on parallel lines with the conjunction on a dotted line between them.

**Example:**　　　Candice and Marisa walked to school.

Directions: Diagram the subjects and predicates in the following sentences, which have either compound subjects or compound predicates.

**1.** Frank and Ernest played in the band.

**2.** Jennifer jumped and ran around the field.

**3.** Peas and carrots are my favorite vegetables.

# Diagramming Predicate Nominatives

The diagram for a **predicate nominative** is very similar to that of the direct object (see page 34). The main difference is a diagonal line that is slanted back towards the subject and separates the predicate nominative from a linking verb.

**Example:** Jessica is a fantastic singer.

| Jessica | is \ singer |
|---------|-------------|

Directions: Diagram the following sentences.

**1.** Cantaloupes are my favorite fruit.

**2.** Patricia has always been a star student.

**3.** Mrs. Allen is the principal of my school.

**4.** My brother is the quarterback of the team.

# Diagramming Predicate Adjectives

Just like the predicate nominative, the **predicate adjective** is written on the main line after the verb and is separated by a slanted line that does not cross the main line.

**Example:** Ballet dancers are skillful performers.

| dancers | are \ performers |

Directions: Diagram the subjects, predicates, and predicate adjectives in the following sentences.

**1.** Hippos can be vicious.

**2.** Bola, a student from Africa, is studious.

**3.** Rap music is very popular.

**4.** This colorful bracelet was a gift from my uncle.

# Sentence Fragments

A group of words that does not express a complete thought is called a **sentence fragment**. A fragment is *not* a sentence.

**Example:** On the counter in the kitchen.
(sentence fragment)

Directions: Identify which groups of words are sentences by writing the letter *S* in the blank. If the group of words does not form a sentence, write *F*.

1. _____ Benjamin, one of my best friends in my class.

2. _____ Emery completed his project in record time.

3. _____ The song that was playing in the background.

4. _____ To understand the problem in math.

5. _____ I have told you over and over to read the directions.

6. _____ Follow the directions carefully before you begin the exercise.

7. _____ Through the air, over the field, and into the pond.

8. _____ On the floor in the dining room behind the buffet.

9. _____ Under the buffet, you will find my sleeping dog.

10. _____ If you can answer all of these questions on time.

11. _____ Where do you think you are going without a pass?

12. _____ The candles were burning, and the music played.

41

# Run-on Sentences

A **run-on sentence** is a sentence that contains two or more sentences that run together.

**Example:** Morgan chased the ball he went to the pool and swam three laps he is very tired.
(*Run-on sentence containing three sentences*)

Notice the three sentences formed from one:
Morgan chased the ball.
He went to the pool and swam three laps.
He is very tired.

Directions: Rewrite the following run-on sentences.

1. Mrs. Talbert is expecting a baby she hopes it's a girl and she bought many baby clothes. _____

   _____

   _____

2. Alexander Graham Bell was born in Scotland his father was a teacher of the deaf. _____

   _____

   _____

3. Louis Armstrong was a trumpeter and vocalist in New Orleans he started performing at the age of seventeen.

   _____

   _____

   _____

4. Albert Einstein became interested in math and science when he was young he changed the world of science.

   _____

   _____

   _____

# Dangling and Misplaced Modifiers

A **dangling modifier** is said to dangle when there isn't any word next to it to modify. A good rule to remember is that if an adjective phrase comes at the beginning of a sentence, it must modify the subject.

**Example:** Running into the kitchen, my telephone began to ring. (Telephones do not run into the kitchen.)

Running into the kitchen, I heard my telephone begin to ring. (Correctly written.)

A **misplaced modifier** is similar to a dangling modifier except that it appears at the middle or end of the sentence.

**Example:** Graham Department Store accepts returns from customers of any size. (Does the store accept any size customer or any size return?)

Graham Department Store accepts returns of any size from customers. (Correctly written.)

Directions: Rewrite the following sentences by correcting the dangling or misplaced modifiers.

**1.** My sister Jamie made brownies for the party dripping with chocolate frosting. _____

_____

**2.** The morning passed quickly reading stories and playing games on my computer. _____

_____

**3.** Rev. Jones explained why stealing is wrong on Sunday.

_____

_____

# Combining Sentences

To combine two short, choppy sentences into a compound sentence, use a comma and a conjunction.

**Example:** Tom bought a new car. He likes it very much.

Tom bought a new car, **and** he likes it very much.

Directions: Using a conjunction and punctuation, combine the simple sentences into one compound sentence.

1. Michael Jordan played for the Bulls. In 1987 he scored 159 points in three games. _____

   _____

   _____

2. Thurgood Marshall was a U.S. Supreme Court justice. He defended constitutional rights. _____

   _____

   _____

3. Robert F. Kennedy was the U.S. attorney general. He was the president's closest advisor. _____

   _____

   _____

4. Muhammad Ali was a boxer who never wanted to quit. Ali has Parkinson's disease. _____

   _____

   _____

5. Albert can play the drums. He can play the trombone.

   _____

   _____

   _____

# Enhancing Sentences

Directions: Since you know how to use adjectives, adverbs, prepositional phrases, conjunctions, and interjections, here's your chance to rewrite the following basic sentences in order to make your sentences more colorful and interesting.

**1.** The rain was falling.

_____

**2.** Ernest Hemingway was an American author.

_____

**3.** Carl's Boatyard is in Michigan.

_____

**4.** Alexandra got a new computer.

_____

**5.** The houses in my neighborhood are expensive.

_____

**6.** To make the basketball team is Richard's goal.

_____

**7.** The tornado destroyed my town.

_____

**8.** Teenagers enjoy driving cars.

_____

# Writing Various Types of Sentences

Directions: Use correct capitalization and punctuation to write an original sentence for each of the four types of sentences: declarative, imperative, interrogative, and exclamatory.

**1.** Declarative:

_____

_____

**2.** Imperative:

_____

_____

**3.** Declarative:

_____

_____

**4.** Exclamatory:

_____

_____

**5.** Interrogative:

_____

_____

**6.** Exclamatory:

_____

_____

**7.** Imperative:

_____

_____

# Reviewing Sentences

Circle the letter of the choice that best describes the sentence below.

1. Before I go to the store to rent a movie.
   A. run-on sentence
   B. declarative sentence
   C. sentence fragment
   D. imperative sentence

2. Marta was interested in studying art.
   A. declarative sentence
   B. imperative sentence
   C. interrogative sentence
   D. exclamatory sentence

3. The cat ran through the yard it leaped over the fence.
   A. run-on sentence
   B. declarative sentence
   C. sentence fragment
   D. imperative sentence

4. When did the photographer tell you he was coming?
   A. declarative sentence
   B. imperative sentence
   C. interrogative sentence
   D. exclamatory sentence

5. Open that jar of peanut butter and make a sandwich.
   A. run-on sentence
   B. declarative sentence
   C. sentence fragment
   D. imperative sentence

47

# Capitalization and Punctuation: Proper Nouns and Adjectives

Capitalize all **proper nouns**. A proper noun is the name of a specific person, place, or thing.

**Example:** Lawrence, Hollywood Drive, Mississippi, Indian Ocean, Valentine's Day, Oakland Street School.

Capitalize all **proper adjectives**. A proper adjective is an adjective that is made from a proper noun.

**Example:** Chinese food, German car, American people

Directions: Circle each letter that should be capitalized.

1. christopher and his dog dexter walked through oakland park on wednesday and then ate mexican food.

2. andrew and his wife melissa went to acworth to purchase a new car at royal motor company which was owned by an italian man.

3. My friend pierre owns a french restaurant on peachtree street in beverly hills, california.

4. The mediterranean sea borders africa, europe, and asia.

5. Many japanese people have migrated to the islands of hawaii because of the many business opportunities.

6. Have you read the latest harry potter adventure story?

7. Our plane landed at kennedy international airport in new york on thursday, february 27, and then we drove to hartford, connecticut.

©RBP Books

# Capitalization and Punctuation: Sentences, Titles, and Quotations

Capitalize the first word in every sentence.

Example: The girl threw the softball across the field.

Capitalize a person's title when it comes *before* a name.

Example: President Bush, Mayor Franklin, Dr. Carter

Capitalize the first word of a direct quote.

Example: Mark said, "Don't forget to read the directions."

Directions: Circle each letter that should be capitalized.

1. mother said, "eat all of your peas and carrots."

2. mayor Davis told senator Clark to assist him with the bill.

3. principal Jones from Lakeside High School presented a plaque to state senator Maria Mendez for her support.

4. judge Julia Jones said, "has the jury reached a verdict?"

5. the town of Auburn praised officer Jenson after his heroic deeds.

6. "welcome to the Fifth Annual Independence Celebration," said representative Anderson.

7. prince Charles of England will arrive at the ceremony to honor dr. Benjamin Ashew.

8. senator Charles Dow is the grandfather of governor Lee.

49

# Capitalization and Punctuation: Periods, Question Marks, and Exclamation Points

> Use a **period** at the end of a declarative or imperative sentence.
>
> **Example:** Open the door for your grandmother.
>
> Use a **question mark** at the end of an interrogative sentence.
>
> **Example:** Will you open the door for your grandmother?
>
> Use an **exclamation mark** at the end of an exclamatory sentence.
>
> **Example:** Watch out, Grandmother!

Directions: Correctly punctuate the following sentences.

1. Have you ever heard of the abolitionist Frederick Douglass

2. Frederick Douglass served as an advisor to President Lincoln

3. Oh my  Did you know that Frederick Douglass was a slave

4. Mr. Douglass was amazed at the wealth of people in the north

5. Did you know Frederick Douglass was a successful lecturer

6. His autobiography, *Narrative of the Life of Frederick Douglass, an American Slave*, became a best-seller

7. In 1847 he began publishing an antislavery paper called *The North Star*

# Capitalization and Punctuation: Commas

A **comma** is used

- to separate words in a series.
  Nadia likes cake, cookies, and brownies.
- after introductory words or phrases.
  After opening the door, she removed her jacket.
- after words of direct address.
  Chandler, please eat your spinach.
- to set off a dependent clause.
  Before Shelly goes shopping, she must clean her room.

Directions: Based on the above comma rules, place commas where needed in the following sentences.

1. "Andrew come here this instant!" said Mother.

2. Well what did you do at school today?

3. As she left for the movie Tracy picked up the mail.

4. You will need flour eggs milk sugar and oil for this recipe.

5. While taking the trash out Joshua saw a rabbit.

6. Singing dancing and playing piano are my favorite activities.

7. In addition I enjoy cooking sewing and baking.

8. Marshall why did you break that lamp?

9. Before you go to your room let's play a game.

10. Yes I think I would enjoy playing a game.

# Capitalization and Punctuation: Addressing an Envelope

Use a **comma** to separate the name of a city from the name of the state or country when writing an address. Do *not* put a comma between the state and the zip code.

**Example:** Mr. Tommy Turtle
321 Crawlalong Lake Road
Murky Water, TN 45658

Directions: Using correct capitalization and punctuation, address the envelopes below.

**1.** From: professor hooter owl
974 hollow tree road
pine forest wa 12943

To: dr albert einstein
e elm sea square
relativity ca 96243

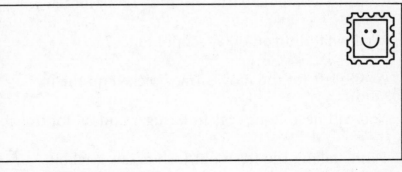

**2.** From: mrs goldie locks
3 bears avenue
too soft ia 45678

To: mrs. peter cottontail
456 bunny trail
hippity hop or 88888

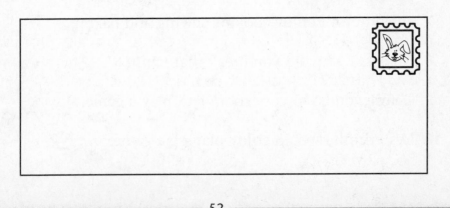

# Capitalization and Punctuation: Interrupters

Use **commas** to set off words or phrases that interrupt or break the flow of thought in a sentence. These include appositives, appositive phrases, and parenthetical expressions or other interrupters that are not necessary to the meaning of the sentence (*therefore, on the other hand, in my opinion, of course, however,* or *obviously*).

**Example:** This computer, in my opinion, is one of the best. (*in my opinion*—parenthetical expression)

Mrs. Thomas, the new music teacher, started teaching yesterday. (*the new music teacher*—appositive phrase)

Directions: Place commas where needed.

1. Kerry my younger brother has joined the Marines.

2. The new principal I've been told is very strict.

3. Hannah however says that he is very nice.

4. Leopold the new French student arrived yesterday.

5. French on the other hand is easier to learn than Spanish.

6. Maya Angelou the American poet continues to speak at various gatherings around the United States.

7. I highly recommend you Mr. Hinton for the new position.

8. The winner of the science fair will undoubtedly be Charlie.

9. Laurence Olivier English actor director and producer was born in Dorking, England in 1907.

# Capitalization and Punctuation: Prepositional Phrases

Use a **comma** following two or more introductory **prepositional phrases**.

**Example:** Across the street in my neighbor's yard, sat a big, yellow cat.

Directions: Insert a comma where needed. If a sentence is correct, do not punctuate.

1. After four months of physical therapy her knees felt normal again.

2. In the summer Angela likes to play outdoors.

3. During the long winter months in Alaska people must entertain themselves indoors.

4. On Wednesday of next week her mother has an appointment with the dentist.

5. Beside the grocery store at the corner of Elm Street and Market Street is a hot dog stand.

6. Under the bridge many homeless people live.

7. In the drawer I found my long-lost necklace.

8. In the dining room on the wall near the kitchen there was a beautiful painting.

# Capitalization and Punctuation: Direct and Indirect Quotations

To enclose a person's exact words, use quotation marks. A **direct quotation** begins with a capital letter. The direct quotation is set apart from the rest of the sentence by commas unless it comes at the end of the sentence. An ending mark is used in that case.

**Example:** Jessica said, "Be sure to eat all of your casserole." (direct quotation)

An **indirect quotation** does not use quotation marks. It is not the exact words of the person speaking.

**Example:** Jessica told me to eat my casserole. (indirect quotation)

Directions: Rewrite the direct quotations as indirect quotations. Rewrite the indirect quotations as direct quotations.

1. "Your new blue dress is too beautiful," said Wanda.

   _____

2. Terri told me that her brother likes Jennifer.

   _____

3. Walter said, "Have you seen my science book?"

   _____

4. "Did you know that today is our parents' anniversary?" said Martha.

   _____

5. Mother told us to get ready quickly so that we can leave.

   _____

6. Mr. Roberts wanted to know who broke his window.

   _____

© RBP Books

# Capitalization and Punctuation: Apostrophes

**Apostrophes** may be used in three ways: (1) to show that letters have been omitted, (2) to show possession, (3) to form the plurals of letters, numbers, and symbols.

**Example:**   **They're** going with us. (omitted letters)

**Matthew's** bicycle is broken. (show possession)

There are two **c's** in *bicycle*. (form plural of letters)

Directions: Rewrite and punctuate the following sentences.

**1.** Jasmines watch was broken when she dropped it.

_____

**2.** Doesnt your sister play the clarinet in the school band?

_____

**3.** Do you know how many *ss* are in Mississippi?

_____

**4.** Why dont you come with us to the movies on Saturday?

_____

**5.** Beths scores on the achievement test have improved.

_____

**6.** Didnt I tell you that Maurices address has three 7s in it?

_____

**7.** The girls basketball coach is Sarahs mother.

_____

**8.** In math class today we learned that there are twelve 6s in 72. _____

_____

# Synonyms

**Synonyms** are words that have similar meanings. Using synonyms helps make your writing more creative and interesting. A thesaurus is a book containing synonyms.

**Example:** big, large, huge, gigantic

Directions: Look at the following words. Choose the word(s) that mean almost the same as the given word. Use a thesaurus if necessary.

1. pause _____ (wait, rush, stop)

2. timid _____ (shy, bashful, coy)

3. brave _____ (daring, bold, firm)

4. friend _____ (crony, chum, foe)

5. fun _____ (mirth, jest, frolic)

Directions: Choose a synonym for the underlined word. Use a thesaurus, if needed.

    asked      brave      pretty      happy      ate

6. The family was <u>glad</u> to help the poor. _____

7. The <u>attractive</u> couple got engaged. _____

8. Angie <u>requested</u> the waiter bring pie. _____

9. The teens <u>devoured</u> the pepperoni pizza. _____

10. Everyone considered him to be <u>valiant</u>. _____

# Antonyms

Antonyms are words that have opposite meanings. Using antonyms helps make your writing more creative and interesting. A thesaurus is a book containing antonyms.

**Example:** big—little; tall—short; straight—crooked

Directions: Choose the letter of the antonym of the underlined word and write the letter on the line.

**1.** ____ The army bravely fought to avoid <u>defeat</u>.
   A. annihilation     B. victory     C. inadequacy

**2.** ____ Cheryl wanted to <u>begin</u> the race in top condition.
   A. halt     B. impel     C. launch

**3.** ____ The little child was <u>anxious</u> to see the little dog.
   A. unexcited     B. concerned     C. apprehensive

**4.** ____ Rich's grades have <u>decreased</u> since school started.
   A. declined     B. dropped     C. improved

**5.** ____ The ballerina danced <u>awkwardly</u> across the stage.
   A. clumsily     B. gracefully     C. ineptly

**6.** ____ Her <u>frown</u> made all the other people feel strange.
   A. scowl     B. grimace     C. smirk

**7.** ____ Andrew and Winston really wanted to <u>leave</u>.
   A. depart     B. vacate     C. tarry

**8.** ____ This <u>common</u> insect lives on the continent of Africa.
   A. unusual     B. prevalent     C. ordinary

# Homonyms or Homophones

A **homonym** or **homophone** is a word with the same pro-
nunciation as another word, but it may be spelled differently
or have a different meaning. Some homonyms are commonly
misused. They include the following:

| | | | |
|---|---|---|---|
| **course** | path of travel | **coarse** | rough |
| **you're** | you are | **your** | belonging to you |
| **allowed** | permitted | **aloud** | spoken |
| **brake** | stopping device | **break** | to split apart |
| **its** | belonging to it | **it's** | it is |

Directions: Underline the correct word(s) in the following
sentences.

**1.** (Your, You're) singing has such a wonderful tone.

**2.** Whenever (your, you're) around the dogs start to bark.

**3.** (Its, It's) not my fault that they don't like me.

**4.** Are you (allowed, aloud) to stay out past midnight?

**5.** This (coarse, course) fabric is perfect for the project.

**6.** Don't (brake, break) the dishes as you put them away.

**7.** I'm not sure if (its, it's) very safe to walk down that alley.

**8.** The golf (coarse, course) was built in 1945.

A **contraction** is one word made from two words. One form of contraction is made with a **verb** + **not**. Another form of contraction is made with a **pronoun** + a **verb**. An **apostrophe** is used to show where letters have been omitted. Remember to make the verb agree with the subject. Agreement errors are sometimes common when using 's with *here*, *there*, and *where*.

**Example:** **Where's** my books? (incorrect because *books* is plural)

**Where are** my books? (correct)

Directions: In the blank, write the two words that make the contraction.

1. He's the captain of the basketball team. _____

2. Did you know he didn't go to practice? _____

3. There's a new Mexican restaurant. _____

4. Where's your father going? _____

5. Won't you help me with this problem? _____

Directions: Underline the correct word in the parentheses.

6. Why (doesn't, don't) they come with us to the party?

7. Why (doesn't, don't) she go to our school?

8. Jody (doesn't, don't) enjoy math class as much as I do.

9. (Doesn't, Don't) you have a copy of the new CD?

10. (Doesn't, Don't) he know how to work that problem?

# Compound Words

Some words form a **compound word** when they are put together.

**Example:** side + walk = sidewalk

Directions: Match a word from Column A with a word from Column B to create a compound word. Write the new word on the line provided.

| Column A | Column B |
|---|---|
| **1.** skate | car |
| **2.** tooth | mint |
| **3.** grand | made |
| **4.** scrap | board |
| **5.** pepper | pan |
| **6.** every | man |
| **7.** table | book |
| **8.** home | spoon |
| **9.** sauce | stone |
| **10.** mile | paste |
| **11.** minute | body |
| **12.** box | mother |

1. _____    7. _____

2. _____    8. _____

3. _____    9. _____

4. _____    10. _____

5. _____    11. _____

6. _____    12. _____

# Double Negatives

When writing sentences, you may use the word *no* or words that mean *no*. A word that makes a sentence mean *no* is a **negative**. The words *no, nobody, no one, nothing, none, nowhere,* and *never* are negatives. The word *not* and contractions made with *not* are also negatives. Never use two negatives together in a sentence.

| Incorrect | Correct |
|---|---|
| We **don't** have **nothing** for dinner that I like. | We **don't** have **anything** for dinner that I like. |
| We're **not** going **nowhere** this summer for vacation. | We're **not** going **anywhere** this summer for vacation. |

Directions: Which word in the parentheses is correct?

1. Connie wasn't (ever, never) going to believe her sister.

2. Walt couldn't go (nowhere, anywhere) until he finished his chores.

3. Jonas didn't (ever, never) want to go to the dentist.

4. Isn't (anybody, nobody) watching the ball game with me?

5. Won't (any, none) of you come to my house for dinner?

6. Not one of us (could, couldn't) sing very well.

7. Can't you think of (any, no) reason to go to the store?

8. Kenny hasn't looked (anywhere, nowhere) for the keys.

9. Why didn't (no one, anyone) tell me the test was cancelled?

# Troublesome Words: *Lend/Borrow, Rise/Raise, Let/Leave*

To **lend** (usually a verb) is "to give the use of."

**Example:** If you borrow books from friends, be prepared to **lend** them yours in return.

To **borrow** is to receive something from a lender.

**Example:** I can **borrow** my brother's car for the trip tomorrow.

**Rise** means "to move upward" or "to go up." It does not take an object.

**Example:** The sun will **rise** in the east.

**Raise** means "to lift up." It usually takes an object.

**Example:** Our sixth grade class will **raise** money for the trip.

Use **let** when you mean "permit."

**Example:** Mother will **let** you go to the movies Saturday.

To **leave** is either "to go away" or "to let stay."

**Example:** Marguerite will **leave** for California tomorrow.

Directions: Underline the correct troublesome word in the following sentences.

1. Dad, please (leave, let) me go to the ball game tonight.

2. Does your temperature (raise, rise) when you have a fever?

3. Samuel, will you (borrow, lend) me five dollars?

4. My grandfather (raised, rose) tomatoes and cantaloupes in his garden.

5. Will your mother (leave, let) you go to the mall tonight?

6. We (rise, raise) at 6:00 A.M. every morning.

7. The neighbors will let Jake (lend, borrow) a hose.

To **teach** means "to instruct" or "to help someone learn."

**Example:** I'll **teach** you how to shoot an arrow.

To **learn** means "to gain knowledge or skill."

**Example:** Charlene will **learn** to recite the poem.

**Loose** means "not fastened" or "not tight."

**Example:** The rope has come **loose** from the tree.

**Lose** means "to be unable to find" or "to fail to keep."

**Example:** The acrobat began to **lose** her balance.

The word **than** introduces the second part of a comparison.

**Example:** I prefer to eat chicken rather **than** red meat.

**Then** means "at that time" or "afterward."

**Example:** Try this dessert; **then** I'll try that one.

Directions: Underline the correct troublesome word in the following sentences.

1. Some coaches (teach, learn) classes in gymnastics.

2. How could you (lose, loose) such a large box?

3. (Than, Then) he saw the wasp nest.

4. A (lose, loose) steering wheel caused him to (lose, loose) control of the car.

5. This chapter (learns, teaches) you how to study fractions.

6. Tree-ripened fruit is usually sweeter (than, then) fruit that is picked green.

7. Young gymnasts can (learn, teach) many techniques.

8. If you let Sparky run (lose, loose) you may (lose, loose) him.

# Troublesome Words: *Accept/Except, Affect/Effect, Quite/Quiet*

To **accept**, usually a verb, means "to take or receive something" or "to consent to something."

**Example:** Jane will **accept** Steve's invitation to the dance.

**Except**, usually a preposition, means "other than" or "but." As a verb, it means "to leave out" or "to omit."

**Example:** I can work any day **except** Sunday.

**Affect** is a verb meaning "to influence."

**Example:** I am usually **affected** by hot weather.

Used as a noun, **effect** means "the result of some action."

**Example:** The **effects** of an earthquake can be devastating.

**Quiet** means "free of noise."

**Example:** The children are too **quiet** in the next room.

**Quite** means "completely, wholly, really."

**Example:** I am **quite** sure they are not up to any mischief.

Directions: Underline the correct troublesome word in the following sentences.

1. Mrs. Drake (accepted, excepted) Paul's explanation.

2. All of us were (quite, quiet) happy with John's decision.

3. The rain had little (affect, effect) on the hikers.

4. Mrs. Sterling won't (accept, except) any new ideas.

5. The woods were (quite, quiet) except for the occasional cry of the wolves.

6. The garden vegetables are (affected, effected) by the number of hours of sunlight.

7. Everyone at the party (accept, except) Tommy enjoyed the pizza.

# Monster Words: Frequently Misspelled Words

The following is a list of frequently misspelled words that you use every day. After you have studied the words in the box, have someone dictate them to you.

| | | | |
|---|---|---|---|
| all right | disappoint | lose | receive |
| athletics | embarrass | loose | secretary |
| believe | excellent | occasion | sentence |
| definite | grammar | occurrence | their |
| describe | hurriedly | pleasant | they're |
| dining | immediate | principal | villain |
| disappear | it's | principle | you're |

Directions: Complete each sentence by writing in one of these frequently misspelled words. You may not use all of the words in the Monster List.

1. Their _____, a _____ man whose _____ stopped writing when he _____ entered, gave us an _____ talk on _____.

2. Quite _____ by the _____, my friend _____ took his sandwich to the _____ room.

3. The _____ doesn't _____ he could _____ the beginning of the play.

4. The _____ shows a definite _____ principle.

5. _____ relieved because the _____ clothes finally _____.

6. It's a coming _____ in which _____ not to be _____.

# Goofy Grammar 1

Directions: You can do this with friends or on your own. Either way it is loads of fun. Simply fill in the blanks below for each story before reading the story. Then, using the words you have chosen, fill in the blanks in the story. Next, read the story aloud with your words.

1. action verb (past tense) _____

2. proper noun (place) _____

3. proper noun (place) _____

4. common noun _____

5. common noun _____

6. action verb (past tense) _____

7. adjective _____

8. adjective _____

9. adverb _____

10. plural noun _____

11. common noun _____

12. common noun _____

13. adjective _____

# Goofy Grammar Story 1

Benjamin Franklin _____ in 1706 in
<br>*action verb (past tense)*

_____, Massachusetts. He had no formal education
<br>*proper noun (place)*

beyond the age of ten. Franklin was celebrated throughout

_____. He was welcomed in any _____ and
<br>*proper noun (place)*          *common noun*

sought out in every _____.
<br>*common noun*

Benjamin Franklin attended grammar school at the age of

eight, but started work at the age of ten. He _____ as
<br>*action verb (past tense)*

a printer for his brother James. Franklin was a _____
<br>*adjective*

reader. He was also inquisitive and _____.
<br>*adjective*

He spent time in Europe and worked _____ and
<br>*adverb*

saved his _____. Then he returned home to set up
<br>*plural noun*

shop as a _____ in Philadelphia. In 1741 he began
<br>*common noun*

publishing *Poor Richard's* _____, a very popular and
<br>*common noun*

influential magazine.

In 1775 he was elected to the

Continental Congress and he played

a(n) _____ part in the
<br>*adjective*

rebellion against Great Britain.

# Goofy Grammar 2

Directions: You can do this with friends or on your own. Either way it is loads of fun. Simply fill in the blanks below for each story before reading the story. Then, using the words you have chosen, fill in the blanks in the story. Next, read the story aloud with your words.

**1.** action verb (past tense) _____

**2.** verb _____

**3.** adjective _____

**4.** plural noun _____

**5.** plural noun _____

**6.** plural noun _____

**7.** adjective _____

**8.** adjective _____

**9.** action verb _____

**10.** action verb _____

**11.** plural noun _____

**12.** adjective _____

**13.** plural noun _____

**14.** plural noun _____

**15.** prepositional phrase _____

**16.** plural noun _____

**17.** prepositional phrase _____

**18.** plural noun _____

## Goofy Grammar 2

Camels _____ thousands of years
<small>action verb (past tense)</small>

ago by traders in southwest Asia. Originally they

were used to _____ across the desert. These days
<small>verb</small>

camels are mainly valued as thoroughbred _____ ani-
<small>adjective</small>

mals in some parts of the world; however, in other places they

are still used to pull _____, turn _____, and
<small>plural noun</small> <small>plural noun</small>

to transport _____ and goods to market.
<small>plural noun</small>

Camels are unpredictable and have a reputation for being

_____ and _____ creatures that
<small>adjective</small> <small>adjective</small>

_____ and _____.
<small>action verb</small> <small>action verb</small>

A camel's _____ are _____, but its hearing
<small>plural noun</small> <small>adjective</small>

is acute. A camel's ears are lined with _____ to keep
<small>plural noun</small>

_____ and dust from blowing into the ear canal. Their
<small>plural noun</small>

eyes are large and are protected

_____ to help keep out the dust and
<small>prepositional phrase</small>

sand. A camel can go five to seven days

with little or no _____ and water.
<small>plural noun</small>

These days camels rely _____ for their
<small>prepositional phrase</small>

preferred food of _____.
<small>plural noun</small>

70

# Goofy Grammar 3

Directions: You can do this with friends or on your own. Either way it is loads of fun. Simply fill in the blanks below for each story before reading the story. Then, using the words you have chosen, fill in the blanks in the story. Next, read the story aloud with your words.

1. adjective _____

2. adjective _____

3. common noun _____

4. adjective _____

5. adjective _____

6. common noun _____

7. plural noun _____

8. adjective _____

9. common noun _____

10. adverb _____

11. adjective _____

12. action verb _____

13. plural noun _____

14. common noun _____

15. action verb _____

16. plural noun _____

17. adjective _____

18. plural noun _____

# Goofy Grammar 3

A shark is a type of _____ fish that is
<br>adjective

characterized by having _____ slits on the side of its
<br>adjective

_____. Most sharks have a(an) _____ body
<br>common noun                                       adjective

with a(an) _____, tapering tail. The pectoral fins lie
<br>adjective

just behind the _____ region.
<br>common noun

There are one or two dorsal _____. The head is
<br>plural noun

prolonged into a snout, and the _____, curved mouth
<br>adjective

lies on the underside. The outer covering of scales is enamel,

and the interior is made of _____. The teeth of sharks
<br>common noun

are modified scales and are replaced _____ as they
<br>adverb

wear out.

Basking sharks and whale sharks are _____, slow-
<br>adjective

moving fishes that _____ by filtering small
<br>action verb

_____ from water entering the _____ as they
<br>plural noun                                          common noun

_____. Hammerhead sharks have
<br>action verb

eyes and _____ at the tips of
<br>plural noun

long, _____
<br>adjective

extensions of the

_____.
<br>plural noun

72

# Answer Pages

## Page 1
1. bear, animal, fur. Bears, scientists, carnivores. Carnivores, animals, meat. Bears, animals. foods, nuts, insects, leaves, fish, fruit. mice, squirrels, animals, fields, forests. bears, equator. continents, Asia, Europe, North America. Bears, Arctic, North Pole. bear, species, South America. bears, Australia, Antarctica, Africa. bear, sleep, hibernation, amounts, food, summer, fat, body. winter, food, bear, den. bears, winter, state, sleeping. bears, areas, winters, dens, time.

## Page 2
1. Parrots   2. feet   3. Parakeet
4. foods   5. United States
6. parakeet   7. Macaws   8. Parrotlets

## Page 3
1. SUBJ = Subir; LV = is; PN = student
2. SUBJ = Harriet Tubman; LV = was; PN = slave
3. SUBJ = Mrs. Allen; LV = is; PN = principal
4. SUBJ = Jasmine, Tiera; LV = were; PN = partners
5. SUBJ = I; LV = am; PN = captain
6. SUBJ = Atlanta Trashers; LV = is; PN = team
7. SUBJ = Mark; LV = will be; PN = president
8. SUBJ = John Glenn; LV = became; PN = astronaut
9. SUBJ = brother; LV = is; PN = analyst
10. SUBJ = Veronica; LV = is; PN = student

## Page 4
Answers will vary.

## Page 5
**Singular:**   3. mouse   4. baby   6. bunch
9. deer   10. child   14. man
**Plural:**   1. cans   2. dishes   5. chairs
7. parties   8. boxes   11. calves   12. trout
13. potatoes

## Page 6
1. B   2. A   3. A   4. A   5. A   6. C

## Page 7
**ANT = Antecedent**   1. he, ANT = Keith
2. their, ANT = boys   3. I, my
4. it, ANT = motor
5. their, they, ANT = family
6. Your, me   7. you; his, ANT = Mr. Thomas

## Page 8
1. her, obj.   2. I, subj.   3. them, obj.
4. He, subj.   5. us, obj.   6. I, subj.
7. You, subj.   8. it, obj.

## Page 9
1. her → father   2. your → CD
3. our → library   4. its → name
5. Their → mother
6. My → brother and sister
7. yours → mess   8. mine → shoes
9. Our → teacher   10. His → team
11. Your → book   12. her → glasses

## Page 10
<u>A</u> tarantula is <u>the common</u> name of <u>a</u> group of <u>large hairy</u> spiders. Tarantulas are found in <u>warm</u> climates such as <u>the southern</u> and <u>western</u> United States and in <u>the</u> Tropics. <u>Some</u> tarantulas may live <u>twenty</u> years or more. <u>The</u> name *tarantula* comes from <u>a</u> wolf spider found near Taranto, Italy.

One of <u>the world's largest</u> spiders is <u>the</u> *bird spider*. Found in South America, it is <u>a</u> type of tarantula. <u>Some</u> bird spiders live in <u>the</u> trees and eat <u>small</u> birds. In Brazil there are <u>some</u> tarantulas that eat <u>small</u> reptiles and amphibians.

Tarantulas found in <u>the</u> U.S. are <u>quiet</u> creatures that live in burrows. <u>The main</u> way <u>these</u> tarantulas have to defend themselves is to fling thousands of <u>microscopic, irritating body</u> hairs into <u>the</u> air by <u>rubbing</u> motions of <u>the hind</u> legs. <u>The</u> bite of <u>these</u> tarantulas is no more <u>dangerous</u> to people than <u>a</u> bee sting.

Grammar Grade 6—RBP013X

# Answer Pages

## Page 11
1. These
2. anybody
3. This
4. that
5. few
6. any
7. many, those, this
8. Several

## Page 12
1. greener, greenest
2. tardier, tardiest
3. sweeter, sweetest
4. stronger, strongest
5. happier, happiest
6. more beautiful, most beautiful
7. stinkier, stinkiest
8. more thankful, most thankful
9. more important, most important
10. more colorful, most colorful
11. littler, littlest
12. angrier, angriest

## Page 13
1. talented → singer
2. delicious → watermelon
3. beautiful → Cynthia
4. wonderful → Gardenias
5. tired → Kenneth
6. angry → children
7. impatient → Nelsey

## Page 14
Louisa May Alcott <u>was</u> an American author. *Little Women*, her best-known book, <u>tells</u> the story of four sisters growing up in New England. Ms. Alcott also <u>worked</u> to gain voting rights for women.

Alcott <u>was</u> <u>born</u> in Germantown, Pennsylvania, but she <u>grew</u> up in Boston and Concord, Massachusetts. Her father <u>was</u> a philosopher and an educational reformer. Many of the family's friends and neighbors <u>were</u> well-known writers, such as Nathaniel Hawthorne and Henry David Thoreau. All of these people <u>influenced</u> Louisa.

Ms. Alcott <u>spent</u> most of her childhood in poverty because her father <u>invested</u> money in many projects that <u>failed</u>. She <u>began</u> to help support the family at an early age by working as a seamstress, a household servant, and a teacher.

Her first book, *Flower Fables*, <u>consisted</u> of fairy stories that she <u>made</u> up to tell one of her students. Her first novel, *Moods*, <u>was</u> <u>published</u> in 1864. In 1867 she <u>became</u> the editor of *Merry's Museum*, a magazine for girls.

## Page 15
1. is = LV
2. lies = AV
3. is = LV
4. has hosted = AV
5. lived = AV
6. built = AV; is = LV
7. killed = AV

## Page 16
1. ate, T
2. meowed, IN
3. instructed, T
4. sang, T
5. is, IN
6. love, T
7. raced, IN
8. ignored, T
9. assigned, T
10. have written, T
11. were chirping, IN

## Page 17
1. was cancelled, PS
2. Will come, F
3. is walking, PR
4. will work, F
5. finished, PS
6. is, PR
7. has, PR
8. enjoyed, PS
9. says, PR

## Page 18
1. future perfect
2. past perfect
3. present perfect
4. past perfect
5. future perfect

## Page 19
A bird of prey is described as a <u>very</u> large bird that usually hunts small animals. Birds of prey have <u>extremely</u> strong curved bills and <u>very</u> strong claws. They are also known as raptors. These birds feed <u>mainly</u> on other vertebrate animals, especially mammals. These birds are <u>primarily</u> predatory but many include carrion or dead animals in their diet. Some feed <u>only</u> on dead animals.

The features common to this group of birds include a <u>very</u> mighty hooked beak. The legs are short and <u>extremely</u> powerful. All of the toes have large, <u>sharply</u> pointed and curved claws. Their vision is <u>particularly</u> acute, and the sense of smell seems to be <u>better</u> developed in carrion-eaters than the others.

# Answer Pages

## Page 20
1. daily      2. very      3. extremely
4. probably   5. most, not
6. truly      7. thoroughly   8. always
9. usually, still

## Page 21
1. best       2. harder      3. well
4. less patient   5. most skillfully
6. slowest    7. most calmly   8. worst

## Page 22
1. C   2. C   3. A   4. C   5. D   6. C   7. D

## Page 23
1. ADV., escaped
2. ADV., was established
3. ADJ., name      4. ADJ., relations
5. ADJ., force     6. ADV., fought

## Page 24
1. During, with      2. in, of
3. of, from, of, of  4. After, of, in
5. Under             6. in
7. of, during        8. in
9. through, in

## Page 25
1. in St. Louis, ADJ.
2. of Atlanta, ADJ.; of the traffic problems, ADV.
3. of the club, ADJ.; with the club emblem, ADJ.
4. to the captain's instructions, ADV.
5. of the western plains, ADJ.; on the buf-falo, ADV.; for food and clothing, ADV
6. of Andorra, ADJ.; on the border, ADV.; between France and Spain, ADJ.
7. In 1783, ADV.; to a height, ADV.; of five hundred feet, ADJ.; in a hot air balloon, ADV.

## Page 26
An owl is a type of bird that usually lives alone and hunts for food at night. The owl has been called the night watchman of our gardens because it eats harmful rodents at night. It is a bird of prey, but it is not thought to be closely related to other birds of prey.

Scientists have identified about 145 species of owls. Owls live throughout the tropical, temperate, and subarctic regions of the world, and they can be found on many oceanic islands.

The eyes of most owls are large and are directed forward, unlike the eyes of most other birds. Most night-hunting owls have either keen vision in the dark, or they have such sensitive hearing that they rely very little on vision. But unlike people, owls can-not move their eyes in their sockets. Thus, they must move their heads to watch a moving object.

The smallest owl, the elf, measures about six inches (15 cm) long, but the largest, the great gray owl, measures about 30 inches (76 cm) long.

## Page 27
Because owls eat mostly mammals, they catch rabbits and squirrels. Owls usually capture their food alive, although some-times they pick up animals that have been recently killed along highways. Some owls hunt birds and insects, while others have been known to take fish from shallow waters. Like hawks, owls tear large prey into pieces when they eat it. If the prey is small enough, they swallow it whole. Since they cough up pellets of bones, fur, scales, and feathers, which they cannot digest, these pellets can be found under their nests.

Since owls do not build elaborate nests, their nests are usually old nests of hawks or crows. Whenever a female owl lays eggs, there are usually three or four, although some lay as few as one or as many as twelve. The eggs are nearly round

# Answer Pages

and are white with a tinge of blue. Male and female owls care for their nests. <u>Because</u> larger owls defend the nests against intruders, they sometimes injure people by striking with their sharp talons.

**Page 28**
Answers will vary.

**Page 29**
Answers will vary.

**Page 30**
1. carpet | is     2. festival | is scheduled

3. I | enjoy

**Page 31**
1. sings    2. has    3. own    4. lives
5. works    6. were    7. have    8. Are
9. make

**Page 32**
1. cookies    2. dishes    3. prize
4. salad    5. test    6. basket
7. Roger    8. camera    9. sandwich
10. note    11. nest    12. money

**Page 33**
1. Harriett    2. John    3. students
4. me    5. Mrs. Drake    6. Denise
7. sister    8. Alicia    9. Suzanne
10. Shawn    11. Mother    12. Alvin

**Page 34**
1. Heather | likes | movies

2. Joseph | bought | bracelet
\ Mary

3. mistake | taught | lesson
\ us

4. actress | handed | envelope
\ him

**Page 35**
1. declarative (.)    2. exclamatory (!)
3. interrogative (?)    4. imperative (.)
5. exclamatory (!)    6. interrogative (?)
7. imperative (.)    8. declarative (.)

**Page 36**
1. You    2. Maurice    3. test
4. You    5. You
6. Jonathan    7. You    8. You
9. Jeffrey

**Page 37**
1. <u>Andrew sang in the choir,</u> (and) <u>he played in the band.</u>
2. <u>I am glad today is Friday,</u> (but) <u>I have many chores to do.</u>
3. <u>Grandpa ate his dinner,</u> (and) <u>then he took a nap.</u>
4. <u>Do you want to see a play,</u> (or) <u>do you want to go to a movie?</u>
5. <u>Jeremy enjoyed the roast,</u> (but) <u>he didn't care for any of the vegetables.</u>
6. The last book I read was *Holes*, and I enjoyed the book.
7. Angelina drank the milk, but it was very sour.
8. Seventy-five percent of the earth is covered by water, and most of it is salt water.
9. Cats make great pets, but sometimes they scratch my sister.

**Page 38**

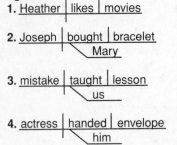

1. Frank \ played / Ernest (and)    2. Jennifer \ jumped / ran (and)

3. Peas \ are / carrots (and)

**Page 39**
1. Cantaloupes | are \ fruit

2. Patricia | has been \ student

3. Mrs. Allen | is \ principal

76

# Answer Pages

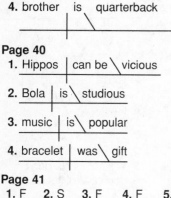

**4.** brother | is \ quarterback

## Page 40
**1.** Hippos | can be \ vicious

**2.** Bola | is \ studious

**3.** music | is \ popular

**4.** bracelet | was \ gift

## Page 41
**1.** F  **2.** S  **3.** F  **4.** F  **5.** S  **6.** S
**7.** F  **8.** F  **9.** S  **10.** F  **11.** S  **12.** S

## Page 42 (Answers will vary.)
1. Mrs. Talbert is expecting a baby. She hopes it's a girl. She bought many baby clothes.
2. Alexander Graham Bell was born in Scotland. His father was a teacher of the deaf.
3. Louis Armstrong was a trumpeter and vocalist in New Orleans. He started performing at the age of seventeen.
4. Albert Einstein became interested in math and science when he was young. He changed the world of science.

## Page 43
1. My sister Jamie made brownies dripping with chocolate frosting for the party.
2. The morning passed quickly as I read stories and played games on my computer.
3. On Sunday, Rev. Jones explained why stealing is wrong.

## Page 44 (Answers will vary.)
1. Michael Jordan played for the Bulls, and in 1987 he scored 159 points in three games.
2. Thurgood Marshall was a U.S. Supreme Court justice, and he defended constitutional rights.
3. Robert F. Kennedy was the U.S. attorney general, and he was the president's closest advisor.
4. Muhammad Ali was a boxer who never wanted to quit, but Ali has Parkinson's disease.
5. Albert can play the drums, or he can play the trombone.

## Page 45
Answers will vary.

## Page 46
Answers will vary.

## Page 47
**1.** C  **2.** A  **3.** A  **4.** C  **5.** D

## Page 48
1. Christopher, Dexter, Oakland Park, Wednesday, Mexican
2. Andrew, Melissa, Acworth, Royal Motor Company, Italian
3. Pierre, French, Peachtree Street, Beverly Hills, California
4. Mediterranean Sea, Africa, Europe, Asia
5. Japanese, Hawaii
6. Harry Potter
7. Kennedy International Airport, New York, Thursday, February, Hartford, Connecticut

## Page 49
**1.** Mother, Eat  **2.** Mayor, Senator
**3.** Principal, State Senator
**4.** Judge, Has  **5.** The, Officer
**6.** Welcome, Representative
**7.** Prince, Dr.  **8.** Senator, Governor

## Page 50
**1.** ?  **2.** .  **3.** !, ?  **4.** .  **5.** ?  **6.** .  **7.** .

## Page 51
**1.** Andrew, come  **2.** Well, what
**3.** movie, Tracy
**4.** flour, eggs, milk, sugar, and
**5.** out, Joshua
**6.** Singing, dancing, and

# Answer Pages

**7.** addition, cooking, sewing, and
**8.** Marshall, why  **9.** room, let's
**10.** Yes, I

## Page 52

Professor Hooter Owl
974 Hollow Tree Road
Pine Forest, WA 12943

Dr. Albert Einstein
E. Elm Sea Square
Relativity, CA 96243

Mrs. Goldie Locks
3 Bears Avenue
Too Soft, IA 45678

Mrs. Peter Cottontail
456 Bunny Trail
Hippity Hop, OR 88888

## Page 53

**1.** Kerry, brother,  **2.** principal, told,
**3.** Hannah, however,  **4.** Leopold, student,
**5.** French, hand,  **6.** Angelou, poet,
**7.** you, Hinton,  **8.** will, undoubtedly,
**9.** Olivier, actor, director, and producer,

## Page 54

**1.** therapy,  **2.** Correct  **3.** Alaska,
**4.** week,  **5.** Correct  **6.** Correct
**7.** Correct  **8.** kitchen,

## Page 55

Answers will vary.

## Page 56

**1.** Jasmine's  **2.** Doesn't
**3.** s's  **4.** don't
**5.** Beth's  **6.** Didn't, Maurice's, 7's
**7.** girls', Sarah's  **8.** 6's

## Page 57

**1.** wait, stop  **2.** shy, bashful, coy
**3.** daring, bold  **4.** crony, chum
**5.** mirth, jest, frolic  **6.** happy
**7.** pretty  **8.** asked
**9.** ate  **10.** brave

## Page 58

**1.** B  **2.** A  **3.** A  **4.** C
**5.** B  **6.** C  **7.** C  **8.** A

## Page 59

**1.** Your  **2.** you're  **3.** It's
**4.** allowed  **5.** coarse  **6.** break
**7.** it's  **8.** course

## Page 60

**1.** He is  **2.** did not  **3.** There is
**4.** Where is  **5.** Will not  **6.** don't
**7.** doesn't  **8.** doesn't  **9.** Don't
**10.** Doesn't

## Page 61

**1.** skateboard  **2.** toothpaste
**3.** grandmother  **4.** scrapbook
**5.** peppermint  **6.** everybody
**7.** tablespoon  **8.** homemade
**9.** saucepan  **10.** milestone
**11.** minuteman  **12.** boxcar

## Page 62

**1.** ever  **2.** anywhere  **3.** ever
**4.** anybody  **5.** any  **6.** could
**7.** any  **8.** anywhere  **9.** anyone

## Page 63

**1.** let  **2.** rise  **3.** lend  **4.** raised
**5.** let  **6.** rise  **7.** borrow

## Page 64

**1.** teach  **2.** lose  **3.** Then
**4.** loose, lose  **5.** teaches  **6.** than
**7.** learn  **8.** loose, lose

## Page 65

**1.** accepted  **2.** quite  **3.** effect
**4.** accept  **5.** quiet  **6.** affected
**7.** except

## Page 66–72

Answers will vary.